To my grandfather, Stanley Haynes, who in 1918 became the first air-to-air photographer in the family.

My thanks to Gibson Carothers, who was an invaluable contributor to the text of this project.

First published in 2006 by Zenith Press, an imprint of MBI Publishing Company, Galtier Plaza, Suite 200, 380 Jackson Street, St. Paul, MN 55101-3885 USA

MBI Publishing Company titles are also available at discounts in bulk quantity for industrial or sales-promotional use. For details write to Special Sales Manager at MBI Publishing Company, Galtier Plaza, Suite 200, 380 Jackson Street, St. Paul, MN 55101-3885 USA

Editors: Steve Gansen and Nicole Edman
Designer: Liz Tufte

Printed in China

Library of Congress Cataloging-in-Publication Data

Haynes, Max.
  Warbirds / by Max Haynes.
    p. cm.
  Includes index.
  ISBN-13: 978-0-7603-2662-6
  ISBN-10: 0-7603-2662-2
  1. Airplanes, Military--Pictorial works.  2. Airplanes, Military--History.  I. Title.
  UG1240.H39 2006
  623.74'60973--dc22

                              2006007053

All photos by author, unless otherwise noted.

**Front cover:** Ollie Crawford in a P-40 Warhawk.

**Frontis:** Barry Hammarback banks his SNJ on approach to Fleming Field in South St. Paul, Minnesota.

**About the Author**
Max Haynes has thirty years of experience as a professional photographer, now specializing in air-to-air. Haynes lives in Maple Grove, Minnesota, with his wife and children.

# Contents

# Introduction

# Introduction

"Clear prop!" With those words of warning, pilot Tim Barzen flips the switch and the prop begins to turn. The starter whines as the blades turn faster until, with a sputter and a cough, the engine roars to life once more. This Harvard Mk-IV, the Canadian-built version of the AT-6, has been firing to life for more than sixty years now. It is literally a flying antique. With the engine warmed up and permission from the tower to depart, Tim pulls onto the runway and pushes the throttle forward. Alongside is the navy's version of the AT-6, an SNJ-4.

Scott Romuld, a highly experienced formation pilot with more than 350 hours of AT-6 flying, has the stick. During World War II, young cadets would spend an average of just 225 hours in training before moving on to other types of aircraft like Mustangs, Flying Fortresses, Sky Trains, and Bird Dogs. Now, more than sixty years later, the vast majority of those fighters, bombers, transporters, and liaison aircraft are gone.

Pulling away from the airport, another AT-6, flown by Chuck Datko, races to join our formation. There are more AT-6s still flying than any other type of World War II aircraft. This is because they were put to use after the war in civilian jobs, like crop dusting. Still, it can be a tricky plane to fly; they didn't call them "advanced trainers" for nothing. The three planes fly in a wide circle so that Bruce Olson, flying the fourth plane in the formation, can cut across the arc and catch up.

The history of flight and the history of warfare have been tied together since 1794, when the French used balloons to spot enemy troops movements. Just eleven years after the Wright brothers made the first powered flight, World War I started, and with it came the first military airplanes. Since then, thousands of aircraft designs have been created to meet the demands of militaries around the world.

This book focuses on planes of war that you can still see flying, still hear their engines roar, and still feel the whoosh as they pass close overhead. These magnificent planes were photographed from the air and the ground, during both airshows and private sessions. Also included are specifications on their most basic characteristics. If you're interested in getting a close-up view of the planes in this book—and the people who make them fly—try planning a trip to an airfield. You can see displays at airports small and large, but here are some of the major airshows in the United States that you should consider attending to see the warbirds included in this book.

The Florida Air Museum's Sun 'n Fun Fly-in starts each year in April. Located in Lakeland, Florida, this show features aircraft from World War I to the present, plus more than 450 booths full of vendors' wares. There are also many seminars you can attend.

Check out a smaller event like the Wings of Freedom show put on every Memorial Day weekend in Red Wing, Minnesota. Smaller shows like this let you get up close and personal with the aircraft. This show also features World War II, Korean War, and Vietnam War veterans who are happy to talk with you about their experiences and the airplanes they flew.

The Experimental Aircraft Association's (EAA) AirVenture event is held in late July in Oshkosh, Wisconsin. For that one week out of the year, this is the busiest airport in the world. There are always several hundred planes to see, with the focus on World War II warbirds. People come from all over the world for this event, and many camp out on the grounds of the facility and stay for the whole week

attending seminars and shows in addition to the daily airshows. AirVenture is *the* place to see the rarest of airplanes as well as history-making aircraft that you won't see anywhere else.

On weekends throughout the summer months, the Old Rhinebeck Aerodrome in Rhinebeck, New York, features flying displays of World War I aircraft and other vintage planes.

In mid-September, the Oceana Airshow holds a huge event of mostly modern aircraft, including a presentation by the Blue Angels. The Naval Air Station Oceana is near Norfolk, Virginia.

On the other side of the country, the Reno National Championship Air Races are held outside of Reno, Nevada, in a spectacular

display of raw power and nerves of steel. The event occurs annually in September.

Don't miss the Commemorative Air Force's (CAF) Airsho in Midland, Texas, in early October. This is an awesome show that focuses on the airplanes and experiences of World War II and features a huge pyrotechnic display.

And to round out your experience, visit the Marine Corps Air Station (MCAS) Miramar Airshow in San Diego, which is held annually in mid-October. The MCAS Airshow is a huge event featuring modern military planes and procedures, including air-to-ground assault demonstrations.

If standing on the ground watching these magnificent planes isn't enough for you, consider taking a ride for yourself and capturing the memory with your own photos. You can buy a history ride in a fighter or a bomber such as the B-25 "Miss Mitchell," operated by the Minnesota Wing CAF in South St. Paul, Minnesota.

You can also join the CAF, or another organization that maintains flying-condition aircraft, and earn yourself a ride through volunteer work. When you go up for a ride, you'll be strapped into your seat with a lap and shoulder harness, so you can feel pretty safe when taking pictures out in the open. In some cases, you may also have a parachute on as an extra precaution. And a parachute is required if the pilot decides to do a roll! If it is safe to do so, slide the canopy forward so that there is nothing between you and the other planes except air to get the best pictures.

Putting the camera to your eye while in the air causes some people to feel a bit queasy. Something about looking through a camera lens and flying at the same time can bring on airsickness, so be prepared. Thinking about all the working aircraft that were scrapped after the war can make you sick, too. Some planes were used for target practice, but most were just cut up into pieces and melted down. It is said that aluminum that started out as frying pans was made into airplanes and then turned back into frying pans.

You can sometimes set up photos by using hand signals to ask the other pilots to move forward or back, up or down. They will try to comply as long as they can keep the camera ship in sight. If a pilot's vision is blocked by the

cowling or wing of another plane, then he will back away until he can reestablish visual contact with the lead ship in the formation. These formations aren't always with other AT-6s, as pictured here. There are many types of vintage military aircraft still flying, but there is nothing quite like flying alongside a B-17 bomber or a P-51 Mustang!

As the flight draws to a close, the planes break away in three-second intervals toward their final approach of the airfield, and another fantastic ride comes to an end.

Photographing "air-to-air" is a great way to get your very own images of these flying pieces of history, but it's certainly not the easiest way. Two of the best airshows for getting ground pictures of old planes are the CAF's annual Airsho in Midland and the EAA's AirVenture in Oshkosh. Often though, small shows held at little airports across the country are the best shows for getting up close to the planes.

Whatever venue you choose, do it soon, because the planes pictured here won't be flying much longer. When the spare parts and rebuilt engines are used up, it will be even more expensive to maintain the planes, and many will just stop flying. In addition, if the oil companies decide to stop making leaded fuel, the planes won't have the right kind of gas for their engines to operate properly. Enjoy the photographs found here and consider getting out there to see these warbirds for yourself. And while you're at it, take a look around you; the heroes of World War II who flew these airplanes and worked on them may be standing by your side.

# World War I: The First Sightings of Warbirds

Stanley Haynes

Norbert Rotter

Andreas Zeitler

# World War I: The First Sightings of Warbirds

On a June morning in 1914, the Archduke Franz Ferdinand and his wife, Sophie, were assassinated while driving through the streets of Sarajevo, Bosnia. This brutal act touched off a world war that consumed the lives of at least sixteen million people. It became known as the war to end all wars.

Although World War I was fought mainly in the trenches and on the water, it also marked the beginning of aviation warfare—battles in the air and attacks from the air. The war started just eleven years after the first successful powered flight had taken place in Kitty Hawk, North Carolina.

After that famous twelve-second flight, the aviation industry actually grew faster in Europe than in America, as did the ideas for the use of airplanes in war. In fact, as late as 1916, two years after the war started, but before America became engaged, the grand total of U.S. military aircraft was just two!

When World War I began, fixed-wing aircraft were used primarily as scouts. Both sides, the Germans, and the British and French, used this form of reconnaissance. They could fly over enemy-held territory and spot troop movements and artillery positions with virtually no risks. The pilots were not armed, nor did they have parachutes. And the planes were made of wood and canvas—clearly vulnerable to fire. They were not designed or made for fighting. In fact, in the very beginning, it was not unusual for enemy pilots to smile and wave to each other as they conducted their business of spying. But that friendliness was short-lived.

As the critical value of the information gained through the air became obvious, both sides began a race to develop fighter planes. These were aircraft with one goal in mind—to stop scouts. It did not take long for the men who flew these planes to become the most talked-about men in the war. Just a little more than a decade after man had spectacularly begun to fly, these daring men were flying and fighting at the same time.

At first, pilots themselves were armed with pistols and rifles. But in 1915, the Germans introduced the Fokker E.I that featured a machine gun synchronized to shoot through the arc of the spinning propeller. The appearance of this airplane is considered by many as the official start of air combat.

Records of "kills" or air victories were not officially compiled. But the fighter pilots themselves kept their own personal count. An "ace" was a pilot with five or more kills.

The most famous fighter pilot of the war was German Manfred von Richthofen, or as he was more famously known, the Red Baron. The baron flew a Fokker D.III triplane. It was powered by a nine-cylinder, air-cooled, 110-horsepower engine. It weighed 1,289 pounds and had a top speed of 103 miles per hour. Equipped with two machine guns, it could reach an altitude just under twenty thousand feet. He painted the fuselage bright red to flaunt his prowess in the air. Before he was himself shot down in 1918, the Red Baron was credited with an amazing eighty victories.

As an indication of the respect Allied forces had for von Richthofen, a British pilot flew over the German aerodrome at Cappy and dropped a note informing the Germans of the baron's death. He was buried in France with full military honors.

By 1918, the skies were contested by superb fighters like the German Fokker D.VII, the French Spad XIII, and the British S.E.5 and Sopwith Camel. These fighters could reach speeds of two hundred miles per hour.

World War I also marked the beginning of aircraft designed for strategic and tactical bombing. At the start of the war, the Germans used clumsy, hydrogen-filled Zeppelins, but quickly discovered they were easy targets. By 1917 the Germans were attacking London with twin-engine Gotha aircraft and the giant four-engine Staaken R.VI, which could carry a bombload of 4,500 pounds.

At the end of the war, the Germans had produced 50,000 planes and the French and British had a combined air force of 125,000 planes. The warbirds had become a mighty flock.

*Andreas Zeitler*

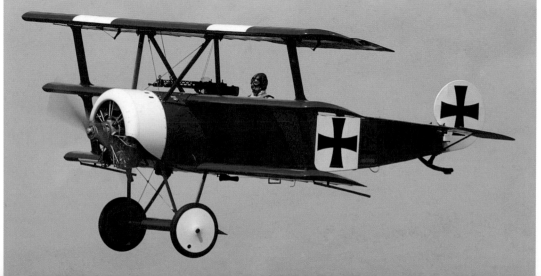

*Left:* One of the deadly qualities of the Fokker was its ability to "hang on its propeller." This allowed it to head up into the sky and shoot at the underbellies of two-seater reconnaissance planes without having to deal with the guns of its victims. *Eric Dumigan*

*Opposite:* This aircraft is flown by the Great War Flying Museum in Brampton, Ontario, Canada, and can be seen dogfighting with the museum's Sopwith ½-Strutter and other planes from World War I. *Eric Dumigan*

*Below:* The D.VII was arguably the best fighter of World War I. It was easier to fly than the Camel and every bit as maneuverable as the Spad. At first, Allied pilots underestimated the plane because it lacked the sleek appearance of other modern fighters of the time. That attitude soon changed as it began knocking plane after plane out of the sky. *Eric Dumigan*

Type: fighter
Maker: Fokker
Country: Germany
Powerplant: one 160-hp
    Mercedes D.IIIa or
    185-hp BMW IIIa
Max. Speed: 116 mph
Service Ceiling: 19,000 ft
Max. Weight: 2,552 lbs
Armament: two 7.92mm
    machine guns
Wingspan: 29 ft 4 in
Length: 23 ft
Height: 9 ft 3 in
Crew: 1

Type: fighter
Maker: Société Anonyme des
    Établissements Nieuport
Country: France
Powerplant: one 160-hp Gnome Monosoupape
    9N 9-cylinder air-cooled rotary
Max. Speed: 122 mph
Service Ceiling: 17,000 ft
Max. Weight: 1,627 lbs
Armament: two Vickers .303-cal. machine guns
Wingspan: 26 ft 9 in
Length: 21 ft
Height: 8 ft 2 in
Crew: 1

*Opposite:* The Nieuport 28 continued to fly after the war and appeared in the *Dawn Patrol* films made in the 1930s in Hollywood. This airplane is flown by the Great War Flying Museum and can be seen flying in airshows in Brampton, Ontario. *Eric Dumigan*

*Left:* Although this was a French-made plane, the Nieuport 28 saw more use by the U.S. Air Service. It was an early favorite of aces like Eddie Rickenbacker because it was the only plane available. He scored twenty-six aerial victories during World War I. *Eric Dumigan*

*Right:* It was fast and maneuverable but had a tendency to shed its upper wing fabric if pulled out of a dive too quickly! Rickenbacker and the 94th Squadron soon moved on to the Spad, which was stronger and heavier. *Eric Dumigan*

# S.E. 5A

Type: fighter
Maker: Royal Aircraft Factory
Country: Great Britain
Powerplant: one Hispano-Suiza engine
Max. Speed: 138 mph
Service Ceiling: 18,500 ft
Max. Weight: 1,988 lbs
Armament: one Vickers machine gun and one
   Lewis on a curved bracket from the cockpit
   to the top wing
Wingspan: 26 ft 8 in
Length: 20 ft 11 in
Height: 9 ft 6 in
Crew: 1

*Above:* The S.E. (Scouting Experimental) was not without its initial problems. One of its designers, Major F. W. Goodden, was killed when the wings of the prototype collapsed in flight. *Eric Dumigan*

*Opposite:* No, the man flying the airplane is not a giant: this replica is built to 80 percent of original size and is flown by the Great War Flying Museum.

*Right:* The S.E. 5A was one of the most successful fighters of World War I and, unlike the treacherous Camel, it was relatively easy to fly. *Eric Dumigan*

*Right:* The famous Sopwith Camel accounted for more aerial victories than any other Allied aircraft during World War I. It was called the Camel because of the humped fairing over its twin machine guns. *Mike Jorgensen*

*Left:* The Camel was a supremely agile fighter but also very hard to learn to fly and prone to spinning out of control at low speeds. Almost as many pilots were killed learning to fly the plane as were killed in combat. *Mike Jorgensen*

Type: fighter
Maker: **Sopwith Aviation Company**
**Country: Great Britain**
**Powerplant: one 130-hp Clerget Maximum**
**Max. Speed: 118 mph**
**Service Ceiling: 19,000 ft**
**Max. Weight: 1,422 lbs**
**Armament: two Vickers .303-cal machine guns**
**Wingspan: 28 ft**
**Length: 18 ft 9 in**
**Height: 8 ft 6 in**
**Crew: 1**

*Opposite:* Canadian ace Roy Brown was flying a Sopwith Camel when he was credited with shooting down Manfred von Richthofen, the Red Baron. *Mike Jorgensen*

*Left:* This is a replica designed and built by Steve Culp of Culp's Specialties located in Shreveport, Louisiana. *Culp's Specialties*

*Opposite:* The Red Baron, Manfred von Richthofen, said of the Pup, "We saw at once that the enemy airplane was superior to ours."

*Below:* The sprightly little Sopwith Pup was a favorite among pilots. It was superior to the Albatros and the Fokker D.III. It was also lighter and much less dangerous to fly than its successor, the Camel. *Culp's Specialties*

| | |
|---|---|
| Type: fighter | Service Ceiling: 18,500 ft |
| Maker: Sopwith Aviation Company | Max. Weight: 1,225 lbs |
| Country: Great Britain | Armament: one Vickers .303-cal machine gun |
| Powerplant: one 80-hp Le Rhône 9C 9-cylinder air-cooled rotary engine | Wingspan: 26 ft 6 in |
| | Length: 20 ft |
| | Height: 9 ft 5 in |
| Max. Speed: 106 mph | Crew: 1 |

# World War II:
# The Warbirds Shine

# World War II:
# The Warbirds Shine

For roughly a decade after World War I ended in 1918, the evolution of military aircraft slowed to a near stop. The German air force had been disbanded by the Treaty of Versailles. The war had taken its toll on both sides.

But by the early 1930s, a new generation of warbirds was in the wings. Both the U.S. and British navies began to build bigger carriers, and new fighters, dive bombers, and torpedo bombers were designed specifically to land and take off from these carriers.

The 1930s also saw an advancement in airplane technology generated by the growth of the airline industry. New airliners, such as the Douglas DC-1, debuted in 1933, featuring a sleek, strong, shiny aluminum body, a more powerful engine, better propellers, and drag-reducing features like retractable landing gear.

It was not long before these new advancements were adopted by warbirds like the Boeing B-17 four-engine bomber, nicknamed the Flying Fortress, which was first flown in 1935. All-metal pursuit aircraft like the

American Curtiss P-36 also emerged as the new style of fighter.

But it took the beginning of World War II in Europe in 1939 to really jump-start the U.S. Army Air Corps. At the start of World War II, America only had 1,900 aircraft, compared to Germany's 4,100, and the U.S. planes were considered inferior, with the exception of the B-17 bomber.

Germany began the war using bombers and fighters to support its rapidly moving armored forces as they marched across Poland, Belgium, the Netherlands, and France. The first application of blitzkrieg (lightning war) was used as the Germans employed 2,500 fighters and bombers to relentlessly attack European cities by day and by night.

In England, the Royal Air Force responded to the German attacks on their cities with the Hawker Hurricane and Supermarine Spitfire interceptors. These superior aircraft, along with the short range of the German Messerschmitt Bf 109 escort fighters, gave the Brits the upper hand. Another major advantage held by the

RAF was the network linking radar stations to command centers that plotted the positions of the German aircraft and radio-guided the British fighters toward their targets.

As the war progressed in Europe, it was U.S. airpower by day and RAF by night. The United States, flying out of England, used the B-17, Consolidated B-24, Republic P-47, North American P-51, and the Lockheed P-38 to ravage German cities.

Tactical airpower was truly the key to victory. Allied forces controlled the skies over Normandy on June 6, 1944—now known as D-day.

But World War II was not just a battle for Europe. On December 7, 1941, Japan executed the biggest surprise attack in air warfare history with their strike on Pearl Harbor, taking out all eight American battleships stationed there. Fortunately, the U.S. carriers were not in the harbor that fateful day.

The immediate U.S. response to Pearl Harbor was led by Lieutenant Colonel Jimmy Doolittle as he led a raid of sixteen B-25 bombers launched from the carrier *Hornet* on the Japanese coast. This was followed by a victory in the Battle of Midway, when U.S. intelligence intercepted Japanese plans to attack the island. In the final stages of the war in the Pacific, B-29 Superfortresses devastated Japanese cities in bombing raids, and after the dropping of atomic bombs on Hiroshima and Nagasaki, the Japanese surrendered on August 14, 1945.

Japan started the war with the world's finest torpedo bomber, the Nakajima B5N2 Type 97, and the finest long-range fighter aircraft, the Mitsubishi A6M2 Type 0 (known as the Zero). But the technological advantage quickly shifted to the American side with the introduction of the Grumman F6F Hellcats and the Vought F4U Corsairs.

Although the fighters and bombers get the glory, it's important not to forget the enormous importance of the aerial workhorses of the war. The Douglas C-47, Douglas C-54, and Curtiss C-46 flew troops and supplies to virtually every corner of the globe.

When World War II ended, the role of warbirds in gaining military superiority was indisputable.

*Right:* Windows over the gunner's position provided a clear view of enemy planes attacking from above.

*Opposite:* The nose of *Spirit of Waco*, flown by the Ranger Wing of the CAF, contains eight .50-caliber machine guns for use as a ground attack aircraft. That's enough firepower to blow up a building or sink a ship.

Type: light attack bomber
Maker: Douglas
Country: USA
Powerplant: two 1,900-hp Pratt & Whitney R-2800-79 Double Wasp radial piston engines
Max. Speed: 373 mph
Range: 1,400 mi
Service Ceiling: 22,096 ft
Max. Weight: 35,000 lbs

Armament: six .50-cal machine guns, two each in nose, dorsal, and ventral positions; and 4,000 lbs of bombs internally
Wingspan: 70 ft
Length: 51 ft 5 in
Height: 18 ft 3 in
Crew: 3

*Below:* Introduced late in World War II, the A-26 was the fastest U.S. bomber of the war. Requiring a crew of just three, the plane flew with a pilot, navigator/bombardier, and a gunner. This is *Lady Liberty*, owned by the CAF.

*Left:* When you see a movie about World War II and it features Japanese fighters, chances are good they will be Zeros. More Zeros were produced than any other wartime Japanese aircraft. The Zero started the war as superior to the planes flown by the Allies and ended the war as losing to more modern designs.

Type: fighter
Maker: Mitsubishi
Country: Japan
Powerplant: one Nakajima NK1C Sakae 12
    14-cylinder air-cooled radial engine
Max. Speed: 332 mph
Range: 1,930 mi
Service Ceiling: 32,810 ft
Max. Weight: 5,313 lbs
Armament: two 7.7mm Type 97 machine guns
    in the fuselage, two wing-mounted 20mm
    Type 99 cannon, and two external
    132 lbs bombs
Wingspan: 39 ft 5 in
Length: 29 ft 9 in
Height: 10 ft
Crew: 1

*Opposite:* This plane was found in New Guinea after the war, partly restored in Russia, and then finished in the United States. More than ten thousand Zeros were produced, but almost all were destroyed during the war or afterward, when Japan was stripped of its air force.

*Below:* This airplane, one of only three Zeros still flying, is maintained by the Southern California Wing of the CAF on loan from David Price and can be seen at the Camarillo Airport.

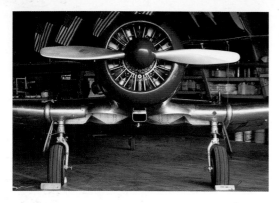

*Left:* Called "the pilot maker," the AT-6 was the plane that more than three hundred thousand American and Allied student pilots used to earn their wings before moving on to other types of aircraft. They were primarily trainers during World War II and are still used to this day for training pilots. Before going on to fly a P-51 or other fighter, pilots had to fly more than 200 hours in a Texan.

Type: two-seat advanced pilot trainer
Maker: North American
Country: USA
Powerplant: 600-hp Pratt & Whitney
   R-1340-47 radial engine
Max. Speed: 205 mph
Range: 750 mi
Service Ceiling: 24,200 ft

Max. Weight: 5,154 lbs
Armament: one forward-mounted
   .30-cal machine gun and one flexible
   rear-mounted .30-cal machine gun
Wingspan: 42 ft
Length: 29 ft
Height: 11 ft 9 in
Crew: 2

*Below:* Chuck Datko flies his SNJ, the Navy version of the AT-6, over the farms of western Minnesota on his way to a fly-in breakfast at tiny Ortonville airport. Chuck is part of a group of fliers called the T-6 Thunder who regularly present shows at small airports.

*Opposite:* Pilot Tim Barzen wears the helmet he used as a navy flight instructor. The T-6 is a great plane for flying in formation, and two more T-6s can be seen in his visor's reflection.

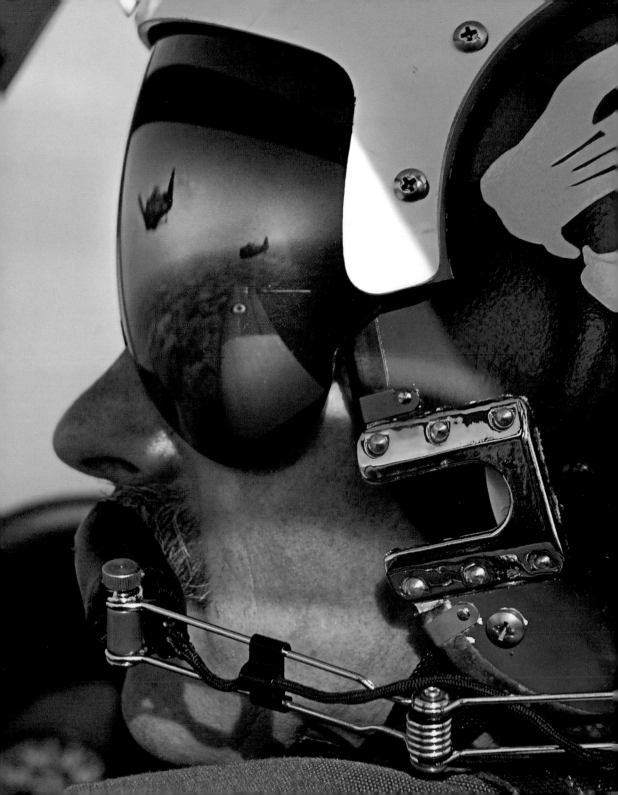

*Above:* You are more likely to see an AT-6 (or as they are more commonly called, a T-6) than any other kind of World War II plane because they were so useful after the war for purposes like crop dusting and because they are fun to fly and relatively affordable to operate. Pilot Tim Barzen flies the Harvard over the Mississippi River wetlands near Red Wing, Minnesota. The plane was taking part in the annual Wings of Freedom airshow put on by the Minnesota Wing of the CAF.

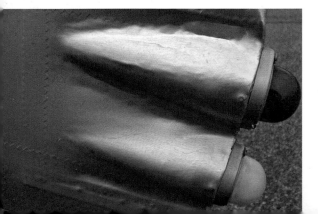

*Left:* The Harvard has a steel-tube fuselage and a fabric covering.

*Opposite:* Pilots Scott Romuld (foreground) and Bruce Olson have been flying in formation for years and can predict each other's movements. Formation flying is the opposite of what you usually do in an airplane; perhaps that is what makes it so thrilling.

# B-17G FLYING FORTRESS

*Opposite:* Rolling down the taxiway at dawn, *Sentimental Journey* prepares for a photo flight. This airplane is based with the Arizona Wing of the CAF in Mesa but travels all over the country each summer from airshow to airshow. You can pay to ride in this piece of flying history.

*Above:* Perhaps the best-known bomber of World War II is the Flying Fortress. Often seen in movies, the B-17 earned its fame flying daylight raids over German industrial targets. While this was effective, it also caused horrific losses. First, they had to contend with German fighter planes strafing machine-gun bullets through the thin metal skin of the fuselage. Then the fighters would bug out, and the antiaircraft guns would begin firing explosive bursts of flak all around the planes. A direct hit or even a close hit could result in a plane going down in flames.

*Above:* A B-17 piloted by Floyd Houdashell.

Type: long-range bomber
Maker: Boeing
Country: USA
Powerplant: four 1,200-hp
    Wright R-1820-97
    Cyclone turbo-charged
    radial piston engines
Max. Speed: 287 mph
Range: 2,000 mi
Service Ceiling: 35,600 ft
Max. Weight: 65,499 lbs
Armament: thirteen .50-cal
    machine guns and 17,637-lb
    maximum bombload
Wingspan: 103 ft 9 in
Length: 74 ft 4 in
Height: 19 ft 1 in
Crew: 9 or 10

*Left:* The smallest member of the crew was the ball turret gunner, who would squeeze into this tiny space once the plane reached unfriendly skies. If the plane broke into pieces, this spot was tight indeed.

*Right:* In the nose of the plane sat the bombardier and the navigator, who would also be called upon to blast away at enemy fighters with .50-caliber machine guns. Just about everybody who flew bombers is now hard of hearing.

*Left:* The tail gunner has the best view out of the crewmembers—unless the plane is being pursued by a Messerschmitt diving down at 350 miles per hour.

*Opposite: Sentimental Journey* flies over Mabee Ranch and the oilfields of West Texas. There were 12,731 of these planes built; 12 of them are flying today and 7 are currently in restoration.

# B-24 LIBERATOR

Type: heavy bomber
Maker: Consolidated
Country: USA
Powerplant: four 1200-hp Pratt & Whitney
    R-1830-43 Twin Wasp radial piston engines
Max. Speed: 300 mph
Range: 2,850 mi
Service Ceiling: 32,500 ft
Max. Weight: 60,000 lbs
Armament: ten .50-cal machine guns and
    8,800-lb maximum internal bombload
Wingspan: 110 ft
Length: 66 ft 4 in
Height: 17 ft 11 in
Crew: 10

*Above: Diamond Lil*, the Liberator owned by the CAF, is stationed out of Midland, Texas, and can be seen by visiting the American Airpower Heritage Museum at the Midland Airport. Its desert pink camouflage paint scheme was used in North Africa. Later in the war, because the German air force had been reduced to tatters, the United States didn't even bother to camouflage their bombers, and the bulk of them were left silver.

*Opposite:* The B-24 was the first bomber with tricycle gear and the first bomber to be able to provide air cover for convoys across the entire Atlantic Ocean.

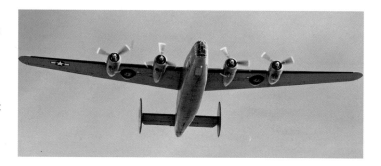

*Above:* More B-24s were built than any other airplane in American military history; more than twenty thousand were completed, and yet there are only two of them still flying today. This is a massive airplane—fully loaded with bombs and ammunition, it weighs as much as two school buses jam-packed with high school football players.

*Left: Diamond Lil* has been with the CAF since 1967 and is the oldest surviving B-24 in existence.

*Right:* To fly a B-25 you need hundreds of hours of experience in other airplanes and many hours flying with an experienced pilot. The *Miss Mitchell* is about a half-second from touching down its nose wheel during a landing at Fleming Field in South St. Paul, Minnesota. The pilots are Joe Grazzini and Tim Jackson, flying for the Minnesota Wing of the CAF.

| | |
|---|---|
| Type: medium bomber | Max. Weight: 28,460 lbs |
| Maker: North American | Armament: five .50-cal. |
| Country: USA | machine guns and |
| Powerplant: two 1,700-hp | 5,000 lbs of bombs |
| Wright R-2600 radial engines | Wingspan: 67 ft 7 in |
| Max. Speed: 272 mph | Length: 52 ft 11 in |
| Range: 1,200 mi | Height: 15 ft 9 in |
| Service Ceiling: 25,000 ft | Crew: 7 |

*Opposite:* With a harvest moon above, the *Miss Mitchell* revs up her engines during a hangar dance.

*Left:* The B-25 gained fame early in the war as the plane chosen to make the first strike on the mainland of Japan. Lieutenant Colonel James Doolittle led a raid of sixteen B-25s from the aircraft carrier *Hornet* to bomb Tokyo and other targets. Dick Cole, seen in the cockpit of the *Miss Mitchell,* was Doolittle's copilot. When asked about the flight, the Raiders said they fully expected to return home safely. To do it, they just had to fly their bombers off the pitching deck of an aircraft carrier and then over the capital city of Japan, make a beeline for the coast of China, bail out of their airplanes, and escape the Japanese troops who were looking for them.

*Below:* An open bomb bay displays a typical rack of bombs. The plane could carry 5,000 pounds—about the weight of a fully grown rhinoceros.

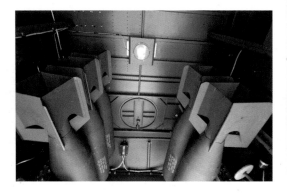

*Previous pages:* The B-25 was flown by the Dutch, British, Chinese, Russian, and Australian militaries, as well the U.S. forces.

*Above:* This is a view of the crawl space leading up to the nose of the aircraft where the bombardier was positioned. If the plane was hit, he would have to crawl back out of this tunnel with his parachute on to exit the plane—no fun!

*Opposite:* The bombardier placed his eye over the rubber eyepiece of the top-secret Norden bombsight to determine when to drop his bombs. While this was taking place, the control of the airplane was in his hands. The Norden bombsight was so top secret that the bombardier was required to remove the sight from the plane after each flight and sleep with it next to his bunk.

*Above:* The nose of the plane offers a spectacular view, unless there are flak bursts going off all around you.

Type: long-range strategic bomber
Maker: Boeing
Country: USA
Powerplant: four 2,200-hp Wright R-3350
    Cyclone turbocharged radial piston engines
Max. Speed: 358 mph
Range: 4,100 mi
Service Ceiling: 30,085 ft
Max. Weight: 141,000 lbs
Armament: two .50-cal machine guns in each of
    four remotely controlled turrets; two .50-cal
    guns or two .50-cal guns and one 20mm
    cannon in the tail. Bombload of 20,000 lbs
Wingspan: 141 ft 3 in
Length: 99 ft
Height: 29 ft 7 in
Crew: 10 or 11

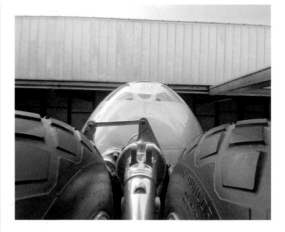

*Above:* The B-29 carried the biggest load of any bomber during World War II. It is a massive airplane that dwarfs the B-25 and the B-17 in size. One B-29 weighs as much as two B-17s.

*Opposite:* While the Superfortress was very technologically advanced for its day, the builders of the airplane never expected it to still be flying sixty years later. The B-29 shown in these images, CAF's *Fifi*, is currently undergoing a massive restoration to keep it in flying condition. It is one of only two that are flyable in the world today, because most of the planes were torn apart for scrap metal after the war.

*Left:* B-29s dropped the first atomic bombs on Hiroshima and Nagasaki. They could fly so high that enemy planes and antiaircraft weapons couldn't reach them.

*Right:* The B-29 was the first pressurized bomber and was able to fly more than four thousand miles, making it the perfect bomber to reach Japanese cities. *Andreas Zeitler*

*Right:* One of the most famous and dreaded planes in the German arsenal was the Bf 109. More than a thousand were at the ready when the war began, and the plane continued to see action throughout the war.
*Andreas Zeitler*

Type: fighter
Maker: Bayerische
    Flugzeugwerke
Country: Germany
Powerplant: one 1,800-hp
    Daimler-Benz DB-605
    inverted V-12 piston engine
Max. Speed: 385 mph
Range: 450 mi

Service Ceiling: 38,500 ft
Max. Weight: 6,945 lbs
Armament: two 13mm MG131
    machine guns and three
    20mm MG151 cannon
Wingspan: 32 ft 7 in
Length: 29 ft 7 in
Height: 11 ft 2 in
Crew: 1

*Opposite:* Although German production of the plane was hampered by Allied bombing, production facilities in Hungary and Austria continued to churn them out. More than thirty-five thousand of the aircraft were built during the war but only about four hundred remained by the end. The luckiest German fighter pilots were shot down, parachuted into the hands of American troops, and spent the rest of the war in a POW camp. The unlucky ones were shot down in German territory and sent back up to fight again.

*Left:* One of the shortcomings of the Bf 109 is the placement of the landing gear. Because the wheels are set close together, there were many accidents landing the airplane.

Type: trainer
Maker: Vultee
Country: USA
Powerplant: one 450-hp
    Pratt & Whitney R-985
Max. Speed: 180 mph
Range: 880 mi
Service Ceiling: 19,400 ft
Max. Weight: 4,227 lbs
Armament: none
Wingspan: 42 ft 2 in
Length: 28 ft 9 in
Height: 12 ft 5 in
Crew: 2

*Above:* The BT-13 is much more complex than the Stearman—it is faster, heavier, and has a more powerful engine. Like the Stearman, it has fixed wheel struts.

*Left:* The Vultee BT-13 was used in the basic or second of three stages in pilot training. It was nicknamed the "Vibrator," not because of cockpit vibrations but because it would vibrate the windows of nearby buildings when it flew overhead.

*Opposite:* This BT-13 is maintained and flown by the Minnesota Wing of the CAF at Fleming Field in South St. Paul. You can go out and visit their hangar museum and see all of their planes most Saturdays throughout the year or by appointment.

*Following pages:* Flown by Craig Rodberg, the Valiant flies over the Wisconsin countryside with its canopy partially open. It can fly with the back seat open to the air. A P-47 Thunderbolt would whiz by as if this plane were standing still.

*Left:* The *Canadian Queen* 3NM is flown by the Ozark Military Museum in Fayetteville, Arkansas. Thousands of hours of restoration went in to transforming an old piece of junk into the plane seen here.

| | |
|---|---|
| Type: navigational trainer, bomber trainer, transport | Service Ceiling: 18,200 ft |
| Maker: Beech | Max. Weight: 9,300 lbs |
| Country: USA | Armament: none |
| Powerplant: two 450-hp Pratt and Whitney R-985s | Wingspan: 47 ft 8 in |
| Max. Speed: 219 mph | Length: 34 ft 2 in |
| Range: 1,140 mi | Height: 9 ft 2 in |
| | Crew: 2 |

*Opposite:* These planes, often more than sixty years old, need constant attention to make sure they are operating safely.

*Following pages:* Ray Plote's AT-11 gleams in the sunlight, a huge expanse of chrome reflecting the American flag.

*Right:* The beautiful Beech C-45 had many names for its many uses during the war. What started out as the Beechcraft Model 18 commercial transport became a bomber trainer (AT-11),a navigation trainer (AT-7), a photo reconnaissance aircraft (F-2), and served in the Royal Canadian Air Force as the 3NM.

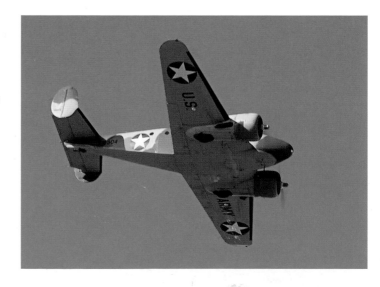

*Above left:* More than one thousand C-47s participated in the D-day invasion of Europe, both as paratroop transports and as glider tugs. A C-47 can transport up to twenty-eight paratroops, fourteen stretchers, or one thousand pounds of cargo. Pilot Doug Rozendaal exits *Duggy*, a C-47 owned by Robert Odegaard and based in Kindred, North Dakota.

*Above right:* The "Gooney Bird" is the military version of the DC-3 and became the most important transport plane of the war. In fact, General Eisenhower called the C-47 one of the four most important weapons of the war, along with the jeep, the bazooka, and the atom bomb.

*Opposite:* The rugged Skytrain was involved in every theater of World War II, and some were even equipped with skis and floats so that the plane could be used practically everywhere. The plane could be compared to the Russian Antonov AN2 Colt.

| | | |
|---|---|---|
| Type: cargo, troop, or paratroop transport, and glider tug | Pratt & Whitney R-1830 radial engines | Max. Weight: 26,000 lbs |
| | Max. speed: 227 mph at 7,497 ft | Armament: none |
| Maker: Douglas | | Wingspan: 95 ft 6 in |
| Country: USA | Range: 1,500 mi | Length: 63 ft 9 in |
| Powerplant: two 1,200-hp | Service Ceiling: 23,196 ft | Height: 17 ft |
| | | Crew: 3 |

*Above:* This plane is operated by the Cavanaugh Flight Museum out of Falcon Field in Addison, Texas. They have a whole collection of airplanes from World War I through the Vietnam era on display.

*Left:* The Wildcat, Hellcat, and Bearcat all look quite similar, but you can tell a Wildcat when it's on the ground by the unusual wheel wells that allow you to see right through the plane.

| | |
|---|---|
| Type: carrier-based fighter | Max. Weight: 7,935 lbs |
| Maker: General Motors (designed by Grumman) | Armament: six fixed .50-cal. Browning air-cooled machine guns and two 250-lb bombs |
| Country: USA | |
| Powerplant: one 1,350-hp Wright R-1820-56 Cyclone 9 radial | Wingspan: 38 ft |
| | Length: 28 ft 11 in |
| Max. Speed: 332 mph | Height: 9 ft 11 in |
| Range: 900 mi | Crew: 1 |
| Service Ceiling: 34,700 ft | |

*Opposite:* The Wildcat was also used by the British, who called it the Martlett. The plane shown is flown by Carter Teeters of the 3rd Pursuit Squadron of the CAF and is painted in the Martlett colors.

*Right:* The Wildcat was Grumman's first production monoplane and a great contributor to the early effort in the Pacific theater of World War II. The Japanese Zero was faster and had more firepower than the Wildcat, but the F4F held its own until the F6F Hellcat took over to beat back the Japanese assault.

*Left:* A variant of the Corsair was the Super Corsair, which was designed to counter the kamikaze planes the Japanese used. It has a huge R-4360-4 Wasp Major 28-cylinder radial engine that delivers 3,500 horsepower. This plane is owned and flown by Bob Odegaard of Odegaard Aviation, a firm that specializes in restoring old warbirds.

| | | |
|---|---|---|
| Type: carrier-based fighter and fighter-bomber<br>Maker: Vought<br>Country: USA<br>Powerplant: one 2,300-hp Pratt & Whitney R-2800-83W | Double Wasp 18-cylinder radial piston engine<br>Max. Speed: 437 mph<br>Range: 300 mi<br>Service Ceiling: 39,500 ft<br>Max. Weight: 19,360 lbs | Armament: four 20mm cannon and up to 4,000 lbs of bombs<br>Wingspan: 41 ft<br>Length: 34 ft 1 in<br>Height: 20 ft 2 in<br>Crew: 1 |

*Opposite:* There are currently thirty-three flying Corsairs but just one Super Corsair.

*Following pages:* The bent-wing shape is clearly seen in this image. This design allowed enough clearance for the huge propeller while still having short and sturdy landing gear for aircraft carrier use.

*Left:* The blazing-fast Corsair belongs in an elite group of fighters from World War II, along with the Spitfire and the Mustang. It had a production run that was longer than any other fighter and served in the Korean War as well as World War II.

*Right:* The folding wings of the Hellcat allowed it to be stored on the decks of carriers in large numbers. While the plane was very useful, after the war it was phased out of service quickly, and the last use of the plane by the United States was as an unmanned flying bomb during the Korean War.

*Opposite:* This plane is flown by the Lone Star Flight Museum based in Galveston, Texas. They have many World War II airplanes on display as well as warbirds from other eras.

*Below:* The scrappy and rugged Hellcat became the best dogfighter of the Pacific theater. It was beefy but fast and agile and could take a beating and still get its pilot back safely to the carrier.

| | |
|---|---|
| Type: carrier-based fighter | Max. Weight: 7,935 lbs |
| Maker: Grumman | Armament: six fixed .50-cal. |
| Country: USA | Browning M2 machine guns |
| Powerplant: one 2,000-hp | and two or three bombs |
| Pratt & Whitney R-2800-10W | up to 2,000 lbs |
| 18-cylinder radial engine | Wingspan: 42 ft 10 in |
| Max. Speed: 380 mph | Length: 33 ft 7 in |
| Range: 1,530 mi with drop tank | Height: 13 ft 1 in |
| Service Ceiling: 37,300 ft | Crew: 1 |

*Opposite:* This Firefly, flown by Captain Eddie Kurdziel, was rescued off a pole in Griffith, New South Wales, and spent nearly a decade in restoration. The plane was awarded Grand Champion in the post–World War II category at Oshkosh Airventure 2002. It is one of only three flyable in the world and is painted in the colors of the Royal Australian Navy. This plane saw action during the Korean War.

*Above:* With its exceptional range, the Firefly holds the distinction of being the first British aircraft to bomb Tokyo.

*Above:* The Firefly was designed for fleet reconnaissance for the United Kingdom's Royal Navy. It was first flown in 1941 but didn't see action until 1943. The wings have radiators mounted on the leading edge to cool the two-staged supercharged engine.

Type: reconnaissance, fighter, and antisubmarine aircraft
Maker: Fairey Aviation
Country: Great Britain
Powerplant: one 2,250-hp Rolls-Royce Griffon 74 V-12 piston engine
Max. Speed: 386 mph
Range: 1,300 mi
Service Ceiling: 28,400 ft
Max. Weight: 16,096 lbs
Armament: four 20mm cannons in wings, and underwing hard points for sixteen 60-lb rockets or two 1,000-lb bombs
Wingspan: 41 ft 2 in
Length: 37 ft 11 in
Height: 14 ft 4 in
Crew: 2

*Left:* The Fw190 ranks with the Spitfire, Corsair, and Mustang as one of the best fighters of the war. It was a ferocious fighting machine with long-range cannons able to blast away at the bombers invading its territory. It was designed to replace the Messerschmitt Bf 109 and was the fastest German fighter of World War II. *Andreas Zeitler*

*Opposite:* The 190 had wide-track landing gear that made landings and takeoffs safer. This was done in response to the problems experienced with the Messerschmitt Bf 109. The Fw190s were excellent fighters, but they were hampered at the end of the war by shortages in parts, gasoline, and experienced pilots. *Norbert Rotter*

| | |
|---|---|
| Type: escort fighter and fighter-bomber | Max. Weight: 10,800 lbs |
| Maker: Focke-Wulf | Armament: two 13mm machine guns and four 20mm cannon or two 20mm and two 30mm cannon |
| Country: German | |
| Powerplant: one 1,700-hp BMW 801D 14-cylinder radial engine | Wingspan: 34 ft 6 in |
| Maximum Speed: 408 mph | Length: 29 ft |
| Range: 560 mi | Height: 13 ft |
| Service Ceiling: 37,400 ft | Crew: 1 |

*Right:* A German deserter flew his plane into Allied hands in 1942, and the plane was studied thoroughly. It influenced the design of Britain's Hawker Fury. *Norbert Rotter*

Type: utility amphibian
Maker: Grumman
Country: USA
Powerplant: one 1,050-hp Wright R-1820-54
    Cyclone 9-cylinder radial piston engine
Max. speed: 190 mph
Range: 850 mi
Service Ceiling: 26,700 ft
Max. Weight: 7,290 lbs
Armament: usually unarmed, although provision
    was made for one 7.62mm machine gun in
    rear cockpit and up to 647 lbs of bombs or
    depth charges
Wingspan: 40 ft
Length: 34 ft
Height: 12 ft 4 in
Crew: 2 or 3

*Above and opposite:* The Duck was the earliest of Grumman's amphibious airplane designs and first flew in 1933. While the awkward shape of the Duck makes it look impractical, it was actually very effective as a ship-to-shore utility aircraft, and more than once found itself in action.against the enemy in the Pacific. After the attack on Pearl Harbor, a single Grumman Duck armed only with the radioman's rifle flew out to look for the Japanese fleet. The J2F served in the coast guard until the early 1950s. The plane shown here is owned and flown by Chuck Greenhill and was Reserve Grand Champion—World War II at Oshkosh in 2005. The plane is based out of Kenosha, Wisconsin.

*Left:* The Widgeon came about after the success of the larger Grumman Goose, when a smaller, lighter plane was needed for medium-range missions guarding the coastlines of the United States.

*Opposite:* This Widgeon is painted in the colors of the Royal Navy.

Type: transport, coastal
   watch, antisubmarine
   aircraft
Maker: Grumman
Country: USA
Powerplant: two 200-hp
   Ranger L-440C-5
   inline engines
Max. Speed: 153 mph
Range: 920 mi
Service Ceiling: 14,600 ft
Max. Weight: 4,500 lbs
Armament: one 325-lb
   depth charge
Wingspan: 40 ft
Length: 31 ft 1 in
Height: 11 ft 5 in
Crew: 2 plus 3 passengers

*Below:* During the war the Germans prowled along the coast of the United States looking for easy targets. Widgeons were used because they could spot the dark shape of the submarine and, if they were lucky, drop a depth charge on it and blow it sky high. A Widgeon was mistakenly credited with sinking a submarine off the coast of Louisiana, but later findings by the coast guard revealed that the sub in question got away.

*Left:* Pilot Steve Zoelle guides the L-5 in for a short-field landing. The plane was especially useful for landing on short, rough fields, picking up litter patients, and doing reconnaissance.

*Opposite:* Sam Tabor's *My Sweet Shari* flies past a Sherman tank at Warbirds North airfield in Spooner, Wisconsin.

*Right:* The ceiling of this L-5 is clear to allow for a greater field of view. Imagine yourself across enemy lines, weaving in and out of clouds and treetops trying to discover troop movements with fighters roaring overhead. It was a good idea to know whose fighters you might be dealing with.

| | |
|---|---|
| Type: light observation aircraft | Service Ceiling: 15,600 ft |
| Maker: Stinson | Max. Weight: 2,054 lbs |
| Country: USA | Armament: none |
| Powerplant: one Lycoming | Wingspan: 34 ft |
| O-435 piston engine | Length: 24 ft 1 in |
| Max. Speed: 130 mph | Height: 9 ft |
| Range: 360 mi | Crew: 1 or 2 |

*Following pages:* Tabor flew *My Sweet Shari* for the filming of the movie *Catch-22*. It has the markings of the "Guinea Short Lines"; this was the nickname given to planes of the 25th Liaison Squadron serving in New Guinea in 1944.

Type: carrier-based
  torpedo bomber
Maker: Nakajima
Country: Japan
Powerplant: one 800-hp
  Nakajima Hikari 2
  9-cylinder air-cooled
  radial engine
Max Speed: 229 mph
Range: 1,237 mi
Service Ceiling: 27,100 ft
Max. Weight: 9,039 lbs
Armament: one .30-cal
  machine gun in rear and
  one 1,764-lb torpedo
  or bomb
Wingspan: 50 ft 11 in
Length: 33 ft 10 in
Height: 12 ft 2 in
Crew: 3

*Above:* Imagine being high above Pearl Harbor on a clear Sunday morning when you see this plane screaming down toward the unsuspecting battleships below. It pulls up at the last minute and drops a torpedo into the shallow water of the harbor that whizzes toward the hull of the USS *Oklahoma*. A huge explosion follows, and the *Oklahoma* rolls over, trapping men inside.

*Left:* This replica of the "Kate," the designation given the B5N by the Allied forces, is flown by the Tora! Tora! Tora! reenactment group of the CAF. It was built from parts of other planes, primarily a T-6 Texan.

*Opposite:* Later in the war, the B5N was credited with sinking the aircraft carriers *Yorktown*, *Lexington*, and *Hornet*. This aircraft, also a replica, is flown by Bill Sugarak.

*Following pages:* Even though 1,150 of the aircraft were built, not a single original B5N exists today. The Tora! Tora! Tora! team travels throughout the United States putting on shows complete with fiery explosions on the ground and dogfights above.

# P-40N WARHAWK

*Left:* The P-40 gained fame with General Chennault's Flying Tigers in service for the Chinese before the United States entered the war. The pilots were from the American Volunteer Group and fought against overwhelming numbers of Japanese fighters to great effect.

| | | |
|---|---|---|
| Type: interceptor and fighter-bomber<br>Maker: Curtiss<br>Country: USA<br>Powerplant: one 1,360-hp Allison V-1710-81 inline piston engine | Max. Speed: 370 mph at 10,035 ft<br>Range: 240 mi<br>Service Ceiling: 38,160 ft<br>Max. Weight: 8,850 lbs<br>Armament: six wing-mounted .50-cal machine guns; | one 500-lb bomb or 430-gallon drop tank under fuselage<br>Wingspan: 37 ft 6 in<br>Length: 33 ft 6 in<br>Height: 12 ft 4 in<br>Crew: 1 |

*Right:* When the war with Japan began, there were more Warhawks in the U.S. arsenal than any other fighter. Despite the fact the Japanese Zeroes and the German Messerschmitts were superior airplanes for dogfighting, the P-40 had a large role to play in the war and was an excellent ground-attack fighter.

*Opposite:* This P-40, flown by Ollie Crawford of the Commemorative Air Force, is painted in the markings of the Flying Tigers' Warhawk No. 48, which was flown by Tex Hill. General Hill shot down twelve Japanese aircraft as leader of the 2nd Squadron, known as the "Panda Bears."

*Previous pages:* There are still twenty-two P-40s flying today. Pictured in this spread is the *Jackie C,* owned by the American Airpower Museum and flown by Jeff Clyman out of Republic Airport in Long Island, New York.

*Right:* In October 2005 the last P-40 pilot who flew in combat during World War II retired from flying the P-40. Ollie Crawford was given a traditional send-off salute by taxiing under fire trucks spraying water above the plane.

*Below:* CAF colonel Crawford had flown this airplane for the past twenty years at airshows and events across the United States.

*Opposite:* Bear Barricklow has been the crew chief for this plane for most of those twenty years. As crew chief he is responsible for making sure the sixty-plus-year-old plane is in top working condition. Because the plane is a single-seat fighter, Mr. Barricklow has never flown in the plane he has so lovingly preserved for nearly two decades.

# P-47 THUNDERBOLT

*Above:* More Thunderbolts were produced than any other U.S. fighter for World War II. That's probably because it was the fastest piston-engine fighter in the world. Although 15,683 were produced, only twelve are now flyable. One of those is *Tarheel Hal,* flown by the Lone Star Flight Museum in Galveston, Texas.

*Below:* Nicknamed "Jug" because of its big bottle shape, the P-47 was loved by the men who flew it, partly because it could take a pounding and still fly back to base. The P-47 was used in all theaters of the war and was very effective as a bomber escort when coupled with drop tanks. The pilots would use the gas in the drop tanks first and then drop the tanks and go after any enemy fighters they spotted.

Type: fighter and fighter-bomber
Maker: Republic
Country: USA
Powerplant: one 2535-hp
Pratt & Whitney R-2800-59W Double Wasp radial piston engine
Max. Speed: 433 mph
Range: 1,900 mi with drop tanks
Service Ceiling: 41,000 ft
Max. Weight: 60,000 lbs
Armament: eight .50-cal wing-mounted machine guns and up to 2,500 lbs of externally mounted bombs or rockets
Wingspan: 40 ft 9 in
Length: 36 ft 2 in
Height: 14 ft 2 in
Crew: 1

*Opposite:* The enormous Pratt & Whitney R-2800 engine was the most powerful engine fitted to a single-engine plane in the whole war. When this plane flies overhead, the tips of the blades make a popping sound as they break the sound barrier.

# P-51C MUSTANG

Type: long-range escort fighter
Maker: North American
Country: USA
Powerplant: one 1,495-hp
    Packard-built Rolls-Royce
Merlin V-1650
Max. Speed: 505 mph
Range: 1,000 mi
Service Ceiling: 41,600 ft
Max. Weight: 12,100 lbs
Armament: four Colt-Browning
    M2 .50-cal machine guns
    and up to 2,000 lbs
    of bombs
Wingspan: 37 ft
Length: 32 ft 3 in
Height: 12 ft 2 in
Crew: 1

*Above:* These first P-51s, fitted with drop tanks, allowed fighter escorts to fly all the way to Berlin to protect the bombers. This changed the whole balance of the war. Hermann Goering, the commander of the German Luftwaffe, reportedly said: "When I saw fighter escorts arriving with the bombers, I knew we had lost the war." These early versions of the P-51 had a "razorback" fuselage that limited visibility from behind.

*Below:* This airplane, the *Tuskegee Airmen,* is named for the famous 99th Fighter Squadron, a segregated squadron of African-American pilots who distinguished themselves by never losing one of their escorted bombers to enemy aircraft, an achievement never equaled. Due in part to the meritorious service of these brave men, the military discontinued segregation soon after the war ended.

*Opposite:* The 99th Squadron painted the tails of their planes red, and bomber groups requested them as escorts. This plane is currently in restoration after an engine failure forced a crash landing. When the restoration is complete, it will be one of only two P-51Cs still flying.

*Left:* The spectacular P-51 is perhaps the most recognized fighter from World War II and has continued to be popular with pilots seeking a very hot example of American World War II airpower. The P-51 has also been a favorite of fliers seeking to compete in the Reno Air Races in the unlimited category, where racers routinely fly at more than five hundred miles per hour.

Type: escort fighter and
    fighter-bomber
Maker: North American
Country: USA
Powerplant: one 1,695-hp
    Packard-built Rolls-Royce
    Merlin V-1650
Max. Speed: 445 mph
Range: 1,000 mi

Service Ceiling: 41,900 ft
Max. Weight: 12,100 lbs
Armament: six .50-cal. machine
    guns and ten 5-in. rockets
    or 2,000 lbs of bombs
Wingspan: 37 ft
Length: 32 ft 3 in
Height: 13 ft 8 in
Crew: 1

*Opposite:* Brigadier General (ret.) Reg Urschler puts *Gunfighter* through its paces over Mabee Ranch in West Texas.

*Right:* The cockpit of *Gunfighter,* flown by the Great Plains Wing of the CAF, has been modified from its original configuration to accommodate modern avionics. Once sold from storage for less than two thousand dollars, a fully restored Mustang like this one is worth more than one million dollars.

*Right: Glamorous Gal* shows off her glamorous nose art and the exhaust stains from her Merlin engine. Originally the P-51 was fitted with an Allison engine that couldn't fly at high altitudes. The Merlin Rolls-Royce engine made the fighter a complete package.

*Left: Red Nose* and *Gunfighter* fly in close formation over the crowds at Airsho 2005. The P-51D gained fame in World War II as a superior fighter that could take on the Focke-Wulfs and Messerschmitts of the German air force.

*Opposite:* Pilot Stan Musick looks back to maintain eye contact while flying in formation. The aircraft is *Red Nose,* flown by the Dixie Wing of the CAF. The P-51 was often counted on to fly as an escort for wounded B-17s trying to make their way back to home airfields in England.

*Following pages:* A Zero replica flown by Tora! Tora! Tora! trails airshow smoke as it is pursued by Reg Urschler and Larry Lumpkin in the P-51D Gunfighter.

*Right:* With the fall of Siam to Japan, the planes were diverted back into U.S. hands.

*Opposite:* More than five hundred different kinds of airplanes were created for use in World War II, and this is one of those designs that that didn't enter into widespread use. Pilot and owner Pat McClure cleans the engine cowling after a long flight.

*Following pages:* The P-64 is essentially a single-place fighter version of the North American NA-16, which is an early version of the AT-6 trainer. Pilot Lenny Shores displays the landing gear of the aircraft.

| Type: two-seat advanced pilot trainer | Max. Speed: 270 mph | Wingspan: 37 ft 3 in |
|---|---|---|
| Maker: North American | Range: 750 mi | Length: 27 ft |
| Country: USA | Service Ceiling: 24,200 ft | Height: 9 ft |
| Powerplant: 600-hp Pratt & Whitney R-1340-47 radial engine | Max. Weight: 6,990 lbs | Crew: 1 |
| | Armament: two .30-cal. machine guns and two 20mm cannon | |

*Left:* Only six P-64s were ever built, making it a very rare airplane. This one is a replica built mostly from an AT-6. They were originally designated as NA-50A fighters built for the Siamese government.

*Above:* The PBY was normally painted a flat blue color with a white underbelly to provide camouflage on water and above it. *Bernard Friel*

*Opposite:* When the PBY made its move to civilian life as a water bomber putting out forest fires, the red color made it easier to see. *Bernard Friel*

Type: long-range maritime patrol bomber and air-sea rescue aircraft
Maker: Consolidated
Country: USA
Powerplant: two 1,200-hp Pratt & Whitney R-1830-92 Twin Wasp radial piston engines
Max. Speed: 179 mph
Range: 2,554 mi
Service Ceiling: 14,698 ft
Max. Weight: 35,419 lbs
Armament: two 7.62mm machine guns in bow, one 7.62mm machine gun firing aft from the hull step, and two .50-cal machine guns in beam position
Wingspan: 104 ft
Length: 63 ft 11 in
Height: 20 ft 2 in
Crew: Up to 9

*Above:* The plane was originally designed for water use only, and the crew attached wheels when the plane needed servicing on land. Later models became true amphibians, like these two planes, which can be seen at the hangar of the CAF's Lake Superior Detachment in Duluth, Minnesota.

*Left:* Among its many nicknames, the Polikarpov was called "Rata" (Rat) by the opposition and "Mosca" (Fly) by those who loved to fly it. It may look like a child's plaything, a cute little airplane with stubby wings and fuselage, but this was no toy—it was a lethal fighting machine.

*Opposite:* The Poli I-16 was the first monoplane fighter with a cantilever wing. It made a huge splash in the aviation world when it was first introduced. It was an advanced marvel when it fought in the Spanish Civil War, but it was already outdated by the time World War II started.

Type: fighter
Maker: State Industries
Country: USSR
Powerplant: one 775-hp
   M.25B 9-cylinder radial
Max. Speed: 288 mph
Range: 497 mi
Service Ceiling: 29,500 ft
Max. Weight: 4,519 lbs
Armament: four machine guns
Wingspan: 29 ft 6 in
Length: 19 ft 11 in
Height: 8 ft 5 in
Crew: 1

*Left:* Designed in 1933, the I-16 was very technologically advanced and sported a huge engine for its size.

# POLIKARPOV I-16

*Left:* Pilot Carter Teeters is one of very few pilots who are qualified to fly this rare airplane owned by the CAF.

*Opposite:* A tiny plane compared to other fighters from World War II, the "Ishak" (Little Donkey) was used by the Russians until phased out by more modern planes in 1942 and 1943.

*Following pages:* The aircraft was also one of the first in the world to feature retractable landing gear and a variable-pitch propeller.

*Below:* The I-16 was built by convict labor in an aircraft factory that doubled as a penitentiary. Not only were the workers convicts, the very talented designers were, too. Dmitri Grigorovich and Nikolai Polikarpov were clapped into irons by Joseph Stalin to make sure they worked as hard as possible to design a modern fighter.

*Left:* This Slow But Deadly dive bomber gained fame from its role in the Battle of Midway, when SBDs wrecked all four of the Japanese carriers in a matter of minutes. This helped turn the tide in the war with Japan.

*Opposite:* The Dauntless is equipped with specialized air brakes, which are deployed to stabilize the plane's speed during high-speed dives and are then retracted so the aircraft can make a speedy getaway.

Type: carrier-based scout plane and dive bomber
Maker: Douglas
Country: USA
Powerplant: one 1,200-hp Wright R-1820-60 Cyclone air-cooled radial piston engine
Max. Speed: 254 mph
Range: 453 mi on a bombing mission, 771 mi on a scouting mission
Service Ceiling: 24,275 ft
Max. Weight: 9,519 lbs

Armament: two .50-cal fixed machine guns in the nose and two 7.62mm manually aimed machine guns in the rear crewman's position, plus up to 1,600 lbs of bombs under the fuselage and 650 lbs of bombs under the wings
Wingspan: 42 ft
Length: 33 ft
Height: 14 ft
Crew: 2

*Right:* Crew chief Mark "Smokey" Schmidt began his career as a marine corps helicopter mechanic before retiring from the military due to an injury. He works on this Dauntless as well as the P-51D *Red Nose* as a volunteer for the Dixie Wing of the CAF.

*Previous pages:* The Dauntless was a good plane for those pilots who were capable of pointing their plane straight into the teeth of a defending aircraft carrier or battleship.

*Right:* The Dauntless features a huge 1,600-pound bomb held by a double-armed cradle. When the bomb was released by the pilot, the cradle swung forward so that the bomb wouldn't hit the propeller.

*Opposite:* The crewman's position could pivot around so that the plane could be defended from the rear by .50-caliber machine guns.

*Below:* Only a few SBDs are still flying. The home field for this plane is Falcon Field outside Atlanta, Georgia. You can arrange to pay for a flight in this aircraft by contacting the Dixie Wing of the CAF.

*Left:* The spectacular Spitfire lives in the hearts of Britons in much the same way the P-51 is beloved by Americans. In its many forms or marks, it was the predominant fighter for the RAF and was used by the Royal Navy in a form called a Seafire.

*Opposite:* The Spitfire earned its fame dueling with the Messerschmitt Bf 109 in the Battle of Britain.

Type: fighter and fighter-bomber
Maker: Vickers Supermarine
Country: Great Britain
Powerplant: one 1,478-hp Rolls-Royce
    Merlin 45 V-12 piston engine
Max. Speed: 369 mph
Range: 1,135 mi
Service Ceiling: 36,500 ft
Max. Weight: 6,417 lbs
Armament: eight 7.7mm Browning machine
    guns, or two cannon and four machine guns,
    or four cannon plus 1,000 lbs of bombs
Wingspan: 36 ft 10 in
Length: 29 ft 11 in
Height: 9 ft 11 in
Crew: 1 or 2

*Above:* The Spitfire was modified constantly throughout the war, and there were more than a dozen different versions of the plane produced.

*Right:* While 22,440 Spitfire/Seafires were built, just 196 have survived and about 51 are in flyable condition. The vast majority of those are in Europe, so Bill Greenwood's TR9 version is an especially welcome sight at U.S. airshows.

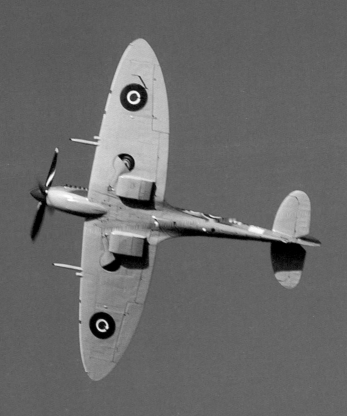

# STEARMAN KAYDET

*Left:* The Stearman is the classic biplane known to most people. It may look like a World War I plane to most, but it wasn't even put into service until ten years after the war. Of the 10,346 built, more than 1,000 of them are still flying! This plane, owned by Paul Ehlen, is a pristine example of what was usually the first airplane any cadet would fly.

*Left:* Called the "Yellow Peril" because of the dangerous nature of flight training, the Stearman is relatively easy to fly but somewhat tricky to land.

*Opposite:* The Stearman was also used by the militaries of many countries, including the Royal Canadian Air Force, who nicknamed it "Kaydet," a name that was adopted by other air forces around the world.

*Below:* Pilot John Sinclair dons a flying helmet typical of the kind worn by pilots training for World War II.

Type: trainer
Maker: Stearman/Boeing
Country: USA
Powerplant: one 220-hp
    Continental W-670
Max. Speed: 104 mph
Range: 260 mi
Service Ceiling: 14,000 ft
Max. Weight: 2,700 lbs
Armament: none
Wingspan: 32 ft 2 in
Length: 24 ft 10 in
Height: 9 ft 2 in
Crew: 2

*Previous pages:* Don't try this at home: aerobatic entertainer John Mohr flies his aircraft sideways over a pond during an airshow demonstration.

*Opposite:* John Mohr and his Stearman can be seen at airshows across the country. Here, he zooms past the wing of the B-25 *Show Me*.

*Above:* The wings are made of wood and fabric, while the body has a welded steel-tube construction covered in fabric.

*Below:* The wings of the Stearman flex when the plane is put into a roll or other aerobatic maneuver.

*Left:* The Avenger is a huge, imposing airplane that first flew in August of 1941, making it a relatively new design for World War II airplanes. It was designed to replace the inadequate TBD Devastator with more power and strength for operations off aircraft carriers. The engine is the same as the kind found in the B-25 Mitchell bomber.

*Opposite:* The wings of the Avenger fold up for efficient storage aboard ship.

Type: carrier-based torpedo bomber
Maker: Grumman/ General Motors
Country: USA
Powerplant: one 1,900-hp Wright R-2600-20 engine
Max. Speed: 267 mph
Range: 1,130 mi

Service Ceiling: 23,400 ft
Max. Weight: 17,327 lbs
Armament: two forward mounted .50-cal machine guns, one .50-cal in the rear gun turret, and one .30-cal in the ventral position underneath the plane facing backward; 2,000 lbs of bombs or one torpedo in the internal bomb bay
Wingspan: 52 ft 2 in; 16 ft with folded wings
Length: 40 ft
Height: 16 ft 5 in
Crew: 3

*Below right:* The Avenger suffered devastating losses at the Battle of Midway but went on to perform admirably through the end of the war. TBMs made the transition into civilian uses as water bombers and crop dusters.

*Below left:* This Avenger shows the early U.S. insignia. The red dot was removed after the war with Japan began because it was thought to be too close in appearance to the Japanese "meatball" symbol.

# Post–World War II:
# The Warbirds Reach
# New Heights

# Post–World War II: The Warbirds Reach New Heights

Unlike the period after World War I, the years following the end of World War II marked the beginning of enormous progress in aviation. Expansive and expensive research and development programs were undertaken in the United States by both the military services and the National Aeronautics and Space Administration (NASA), which was founded in 1958.

The most important technical development to change aviation after the war actually emerged prior to the war's conclusion. British engineer Frank Whittle and German engineer Hans von Ohain almost simultaneously produced the first turbojet engine. On August 27, 1939, the German Heinkel 178 became the first jet-powered aircraft to fly. The first operational jet, the German Messerschmitt Me 262, entered service in late 1944.

By 1951, aircraft designers in the United States, often working with German engineers recruited to America after the war, were developing jet fighters that could exceed the speed of sound in level flight—760 miles per hour. Two such planes were the Douglas D-558-2 Skyrocket and the Bell X-1. By 1953, Kelly Johnson had outlined the Lockheed 83, an aircraft with a new J79 engine able to reach Mach 2—twice the speed of sound. And by 1954, the monster FX-103 fighter reached Mach 3.7—2,447 miles per hour! Even carrier planes like the Chance Vought F-8 Crusader could reach speeds of one thousand miles per hour, and the F-8 was the first plane to cross the United States from coast to coast at supersonic speeds. In 1956, the X-15, America's best-known research aircraft, reached speeds in excess of four thousand miles per hour and altitudes of up to 350,000 feet. No aircraft designed to operate solely within the atmosphere has ever flown faster.

Aviation research and development showed no signs of slowing down in the 1960s. The McDonnell F-4 Phantom II broke more than twelve records for speed and rate of climb. The Boeing B-52 Stratofortress was the first eight-engine bomber with a 6,000-mile range. The B-52 also benefited from another important post–World War II advancement: the ability to refuel in midair.

After the turbojet, the next most important aviation advancement after World War II was the helicopter. Russian-born American engineer Igor Sikorsky flew the first truly practical helicopter in 1939. The first real combat use of the copter was during the Korean War, when they were used to rescue downed pilots and carry the wounded from the battlefield to field hospitals.

In the 1950s helicopter performance advanced dramatically with the introduction of compact, light, and powerful engines based on jet technology. The first was the Bell UH-1 "Huey." Produced by the thousands, the Huey was a huge contributor to the U.S. effort in Vietnam. Later in that war, a more sophisticated version, the Huey Cobra, revolutionized the conduct of air-ground battles due to its ability to destroy enemy tanks without being vulnerable to the tanks' weapons.

Since World War II, research and development activities in aviation have extended into nearly every aspect of science. Experimental aircraft have been created to explore new frontiers in aerodynamics, materials, and performance. Aviation research and development have moved almost as fast as the planes they have produced.

*Left:* The AC-47 had several nicknames: Spooky, Dragonship, and Puff the Magic Dragon. It was a gunship designed to protect ground troops holding positions from enemy advances.

*Right:* The AC-47 is a variant of the C-47. While the original design was a transport plane in World War II, the AC-47 was a nightmare on wings for its enemies and was used in the Vietnam War twenty-plus years later. This plane, *Puff*, is owned by Daryl Massman.

Type: counter insurgency gunship, close air support
Maker: Douglas
Country: USA
Powerplant: two 1,100-hp Pratt & Whitney R-1830-90D Twin Wasp radial engines
Max. speed: 232 mph
Range: 1,600 mi

Service Ceiling: 25,000 ft
Max. Weight: 33,000 lbs
Armament: three fuselage-mounted .30-cal Gatling miniguns
Wingspan: 95 ft 6 in
Length: 64 ft 5 in
Height: 16 ft 11 in
Crew: 8

*Opposite:* The guns of the aircraft were mounted on one side of the plane and fired down into the jungle as the plane banked over the target. Copilot Bill Cowden sits in the upper escape hatch as pilot Mike Connell looks on from inside the cockpit.

# A-1H SKYRAIDER

*Right:* The Skyraider was considered obsolete shortly after it came out, but it went on to serve in Korea as a ground-attack aircraft and in Vietnam as a carrier-based attack bomber. This was because it could fly slow and low and was able to better support the troops on the ground than the high-flying jets. John Lohmar taxies Eric Downing's A-1 into the Wings of Freedom airshow in Red Wing, Minnesota.

Type: carrier-based attack bomber
Maker: Douglas
Country: USA
Powerplant: one 2,700-hp Wright R-3350-26WA 18-cylinder radial piston engine
Max. Speed: 322 mph
Range: 1,243 mi
Service Ceiling: 28,494 ft
Max. Weight: 25,000 lbs

Armament: four wing-mounted 20mm M3 cannons with 200 rounds per gun and up to 8,000 lbs of bombs or rockets on one underfuselage and 14 underwing hardpoints
Wingspan: 50 ft
Length: 38 ft 10 in
Height: 15 ft 7 in
Crew: 1

*Opposite: Naked Fanny,* flown by Mike Schloss, demonstrates the beefy structure of the Skyraider, an aircraft that could take a severe pounding from ground fire and still bring its pilot back safely.

*Left:* The A-1 *Marlene* makes a bombing run over the CAF Midland Airsho to demonstrate how the aircraft was set up to drop small nuclear bombs and then fly up and out of the blast area.

*Right:* The An-2 is the world's biggest biplane. This lumbering giant was built in Russia, Poland, and China. A very rugged airplane, it has been serving air forces for more than fifty years and is still being used today.

*Opposite:* It is one of the very few airplanes that has round windows for the passengers to look out of.

*Below:* The Colt is certainly a throwback to another era, but it is still useful for its large cargo capacity and ability to make short takeoffs and landings.

Type: paratroop transport, glider tug, navigation trainer, utility transport, and light bomber
Maker: Antonov
Country: Russia
Powerplant: one 1,000-hp Shvetsov Ash-62IR radial piston engine

Max. Speed: 160 mph
Range: 560 mi
Service Ceiling: 14,425 ft
Max. Weight: 12,125 lbs
Armament: none
Wingspan: 59 ft 7 in
Length: 41 ft 10 in
Height: 13 ft 2 in
Crew: 3

*Left:* The Colt has had many jobs over its lifetime. It was originally built for the Ministry of Agriculture and Forestry and has served fighting forest fires as a water bomber as well as a platform for smoke jumpers. It has also been fitted with floats for water and skis for snow.

*Opposite:* The Colt saw action in the Korean War, where it proved useful because it was so slow! U.S. jets couldn't slow down enough to be effective against it.

*Below:* This Colt is flown by the 3rd Pursuit Squadron of the CAF, and its home base is Cable Airport in Upland, California. Crew chief John Varley hooks the *Big Panda* onto a tug to move it across the airfield ramp.

Type: trainer
Maker: deHavilland
Countries: Great Britain and Canada
Powerplant: one 145-hp deHavilland Gypsy Major 8 inline piston engine
Max. Speed: 133 mph
Range: 280 mi
Service Ceiling: 15,800 ft
Max. Weight: 2,394 lbs
Armament: none
Wingspan: 34 ft 4in
Length: 25 ft 5 in
Height: 7 ft
Crew: 1 or 2

*Above:* The British version, seen in both of these examples, featured a sliding, multipaneled canopy and was fully aerobatic. It's a nimble aircraft that can do rolls and loops with ease.

*Opposite:* The Chipmunk has a shotgun-shell-cartridge starting system for the engine. This aircraft is owned by Alan Klapmeier and can be seen flying out of Duluth, Minnesota.

*Right:* The Chipmunk, also known as the "flying sardine," was developed just after World War II to serve the RCAF and RAF as their primary trainer aircraft. It replaced the Tiger Moth, a biplane design developed in the early 1930s.

# F-4 PHANTOM II

Type: carrier borne interceptor
Maker: McDonnell
     (later McDonnell Douglas)
Country: USA
Powerplant: two 17,920-lb-
     thrust General Electric J79
     8A afterburning turbojets
Max. Speed: 1,482 mph
Range: 2,294 mi
Service Ceiling: 71,000 ft
Weight Empty: 2,625 lbs
Max. Weight: 54,485 lbs
Armament: four AIM-7
     Sparrow medium-range
     and four AIM-9 Sidewinder
     short-range air-to-air
     missiles
Wingspan: 38 ft 5 in
Length: 58 ft 3 in
Height: 16 ft 3 in
Crew: 2

*Above:* What the P-51 was to World War II, the Phantom was to the Vietnam War. It was the biggest, baddest, most powerful fighter in the sky during its reign. This plane flew faster and higher than any operational warplane had ever flown.

*Opposite:* Variants of the Phantom retired from service as late as 1995 after seeing action in the first Gulf War. Now some of the remaining F-4s are being used for remote-controlled target practice and are blown to smithereens by F-16s and F-18s.

*Below:* The Phantom faced the North Vietnamese MiG-17 and MiG-21 aircraft and fought very well. It often had to make its way back onto the pitching deck of an aircraft carrier, sometimes at night and in bad weather.

*Left:* This plane, flown by the Southern California Wing of the CAF, can be seen at the Camarillo Airport. If you would like to buy your own Bearcat you can pick one up for a mere 1.7 million dollars. Sorry, there's no back seat.

Type: carrier-based fighter-bomber
Maker: Grumman
Country: USA
Powerplant: one 2100-hp Pratt & Whitney
    R-2800-22W 18-cylinder radial engine
Max. Speed: 421 mph
Range: 1,103 mi
Service Ceiling: 34,690 ft
Max. Weight: 12,921 lbs
Armament: four .50-cal Colt-Browning M2
    machine guns or four 20mm cannon, plus
    one 1,600-lb bomb or two 1,000-lb bombs
Wingspan: 35 ft 10 in
Length: 28 ft 3 in
Height: 13 ft 10 in
Crew: 1

*Right:* The Bearcat appeared too late to see action in World War II and was soon outpaced by jet fighters, but it was a spectacular fighter for its kind, one of the best performing aircraft of its class ever produced.

*Opposite:* The Bearcat has found a lot of fans in the air racing community because of its strong airframe and fast engine. You can see modified Bearcats flying against P-51s and Sea Furies in the unlimited category at the Reno Air Races in Reno, Nevada, each fall.

*Opposite:* The FJ-4B Fury is the navy's version of the F-86 Sabre. Although the two planes didn't always share much in common during their development, they ended up with very similar machines at the end of their runs.

*Above:* During the Korean War there was an area of the skies called MiG Alley. Here the Sabre would meet its match—the MiG-15 flown by experienced Russian pilots. The Sabres and FJ-4B Furies were the only planes allowed to go into this airspace, since all other planes were considered too vulnerable. Flying this F-86 is Dale "Snort" Snodgrass. Snort flew F-14 Tomcats and was the navy's fighter pilot of the year in 1986.

**Type:** carrier borne fighter (FJ-4B); fighter (F-86)
**Maker:** North American
**Country:** USA
**Powerplant:** one 7,500-lb-thrust afterburning General Electric J47-GE-17B or J47-GE-33 turbojet
**Max. Speed:** 707 mph
**Range:** 835 mi
**Service Ceiling:** 45,600 ft
**Max. Weight:** 17,100 lbs
**Armament:** six .50-cal machine guns and eight 5-in rockets or 2,000 lbs of bombs
**Wingspan:** 37 ft 1 in
**Length:** 40 ft 4 in
**Height:** 15 ft 0 in
**Crew:** 1

*Below:* The Fury has one element very different from the Sabre: it can fold its wings. It was used by the navy on carriers throughout the Korean War. There are now only about twenty flying Sabres and only one Fury. The Fury can be seen at the Driggs, Idaho, Airport.

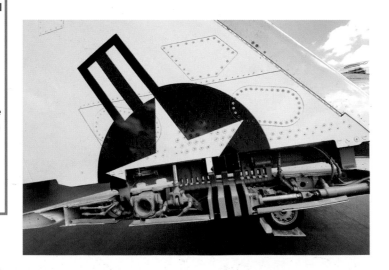

Type: liaison, reconnaissance,
and light cargo aircraft
Maker: Ryan Aeronautical
Company
Country: USA
Powerplant: one 185-hp
Continental O-470-7
Max. Speed: 163 mph
Range: 700 mi
Service Ceiling: 11,000 ft
Max. Weight: 2,950 lbs
Armament: none
Wingspan: 33 ft 5 in
Length: 27 ft 4 in
Height: 8 ft 7 in
Crew: 1 plus 3 passengers

*Above:* The L-17 began its career with the military in 1946 and served until the early 1960s. Originally built by North American, Ryan Aeronautical Company obtained the rights to build the aircraft.

*Opposite:* This nose art was painted by the plane's pilot, David Peter.

*Below:* While production ceased in 1949, the Navion became popular with civilian pilots who have collected the few remaining examples and restored them to their former condition.

*Above:* The Mohawk began it's career in the military in 1959 and was finally phased out in 1996 after a very long military life of thirty-seven years.

*Opposite:* The doors of the Mohawk swing up for easy exit by the pilots.

*Below:* It is a unique aircraft with a triple fin and rudder arrangement. During the Vietnam War it was used for electronic intelligence work and usually flew with a huge SLAR (side-looking airborne radar) pod off the right side of the fuselage.

**Type:** reconnaissance and
liaison aircraft
**Maker:** Grumman
**Country:** USA
**Powerplant:** two 1,400-hp
Avco Lycoming T53-L-701
turboprops
**Max. Speed:** 296 mph
**Range:** 1,020 mi
**Service Ceiling:** 30,300 ft
**Max. Weight:** 19,188 lbs
**Armament:** usually none
**Wingspan:** 48 ft
**Length:** 41 ft
**Height:** 12 ft 8 in
**Crew:** 2

# P-82 TWIN MUSTANG

*Left:* What is better than a Mustang? Two Mustangs! But the P-82 is more than just a bizarre fantasy of some general. It was actually a totally new wing design that used two P-51 fuselage shapes. With two pilots, the plane could travel for more than eight hours to complete its mission. This aircraft was conceived in 1943 for long-range missions escorting B-29s over Japan but was put on the back burner when U.S. forces took control of islands closer to Japan. It saw action in the Korean War, where it scored the war's first aerial victory.

*Below:* Often used as a night fighter, the P-82 could be equipped with a large fuselage pod under the wings to house a radar system. The plane could be flown from either cockpit, but only the left-hand cockpit had full instrumentation.

Type: twin-engine
   long-range fighter
Maker: North American
Country: USA
Powerplant: two 1600-hp
   Allison V-12 piston engines
Max. Speed: 475 mph
Range: 2,240 mi
Service Ceiling: 42,200 ft
Max. Weight: 25,538 lbs
Armament: six .50-cal machine
   guns standard, eight
   additional .50-cal machine
   guns in special center
   section nacelle, five rocket-
   launching racks carrying
   five rockets each; other
   alternate payload:
   7,200 lbs of bombs,
   photographic nacelle, or
   2,000-lb torpedo
Wingspan: 51 ft 3 in
Length: 42 ft 5 in
Height: 13 ft 10 in
Crew: 2

*Opposite:* The plane had a short life in terms of its war service. It was replaced by the F3D Skyknight jet after only a few months of the Korean War. Still, it had some impressive abilities: it could climb at a rate of 4,000 feet (the height of three Empire State Buildings) per minute.

*Following pages:* This plane is currently in restoration. There are no flying P-82s at this time, and only five have survived, making it a very rare airplane.

Type: antisubmarine
   warfare aircraft
Maker: Grumman
Country: USA
Powerplant: two 1,525-hp
   Wright R-1820-82WA
   piston engines
Max. Speed: 370 mph at
   10,035 ft
Range: 841 mi
Service Ceiling: 38,160 ft
Max. Weight: 26,000 lbs
Armament: up to 4,800 lbs
   of rockets, depth charges,
   or torpedoes
Wingspan: 68 ft 8 in
Length: 42 ft
Height: 16 ft 3 in
Crew: 4

*Above:* The Tracker's tightly folded wings made it highly effective for use on carriers. It saw service in many foreign air forces, including Argentina, Peru, and the Netherlands.

*Opposite:* Crew chief Craig Duck signals the pilot as the plane fires up its engines. This Tracker is flown by the Old Dominion Squadron of the CAF and can be seen at the Hampton Roads Executive Airport in Virginia.

*Right:* The "Stoof" was particularly useful because it could perform two different functions in one aircraft: it could both find submarines and sink them. First produced in 1954, it saw extensive service during the Vietnam War and was used by the U.S. Navy for twenty-five years.

*Right:* Steve Patterson's Sea Fury zips across the airspace of the Wings of Freedom Airshow. The Sea Fury is quite possibly the fastest plane to come out of World War II, and this particular plane has performed well at the Reno Air Races, where it rips around the course at well more than four hundred miles per hour.

*Opposite:* The navalized version of the aircraft with its folding wings didn't come into production until 1947, and was thus too late for the war effort. It did serve throughout the Korean War despite the advances into jet aircraft that were made at the time.

*Below:* The Hawker Sea Fury was designed with the aid of German expertise. A Focke-Wulf 190A-3 landed in England and was studied extensively by the British. The Sea Fury's designers incorporated some of the elements of the brilliant 190 design into the airplane.

Type: fighter
Maker: Hawker
Country: Great Britain
Powerplant: one 2,500-hp
    Wright 3350 engine
Max. Speed: 430 mph
Range: 600 mi
Service Ceiling: 35,000 ft
Max. Weight: 4,264 lbs
Armament: four 20mm
    cannon in the wings,
    with underwing racks for
    eight 60-lb rockets or
    two bombs
Wingspan: 38 ft
Length: 35 ft
Height: 15 ft
Crew: 1

Type: long-range maritime patrol aircraft
Maker: Avro
Country: Great Britain
Powerplant: four 2,455-hp Rolls-Royce Griffon 57A inline piston engines
Max. Speed: 302 mph
Range: 3,660 mi
Service Ceiling: 19,200 ft
Max. Weight: 98,000 lbs
Armament: two 20mm cannons in the nose, two in a dorsal turret, and two machine guns in the tail, plus up to 10,000 lbs of weapons in the bomb bay
Wingspan: 119 ft 10 in
Length: 92 ft 6 in
Height: 23 ft 4 in
Crew: 10

*Above:* Contrarotating propellers are one of the unique features of the Shackleton, which has four engines but eight propellers. It was named for an intrepid explorer of the South Pole, Ernest Shackleton.

*Left:* A large dome on the chin of the plane held a "guppy" radar unit so the plane could be used as an airborne early warning system.

*Opposite:* The Shackleton flies past a huge explosion of gas set off by the Explosive Ordnance Detachment of the CAF at the airshow held each October in Midland, Texas.

Type: trainer/counter
    insurgency aircraft
Maker: North American
Country: USA
Powerplant: one 1,425-hp
    Wright Cyclone R-1820-86
    radial piston engine
Max. Speed: 343 mph
Range: 1,060 mi
Service Ceiling: 35,500 ft
Max. Weight: 8,500 lbs
Armament: none
Wingspan: 40 ft 1 in
Length: 33 ft
Height: 12 ft 8 in
Crew: 2

*Above:* The Trojan started out its life as a replacement for the aging AT-6 trainers but went on to serve in Vietnam as a COIN (counter insurgency) aircraft. Pilot Walt Fricke taxies his T-28 onto the runway of the Red Wing, Minnesota, Airport.

*Below:* This Trojan is owned and flown by Keith Baker and has won four major awards for its attention to detail and quality restoration. You can pick up a T-28 for about $250,000, but it wouldn't be as nice as this bird.

*Opposite:* Walt Fricke soars above the clouds in his T-28. Notice the tail hook that would allow the plane to operate off of carriers. The T-28 was pulled from service during the Vietnam conflict when two planes shed their wings from the stresses of combat flying.

*Following pages:* Walt Fricke banks above Lake Superior as an ore boat steams below.

Type: trainer
Maker: Yakovlev/Nanchang
Countries: Russia and China
Powerplant: one 260-hp
    Ivchenko AI-14R radial
    engine or 285-hp Quzhou
    Huosai-6A HS6A
Max. Speed: 230 mph
Range: 450 mi
Service Ceiling: 17,000 ft
Max. Weight: 7,935 lbs
Armament: none
Wingspan: 33 ft 4 in
Length: 27 ft 8 in
Height: 10 ft 6 in
Crew: 1 or 2

*Above:* Built by the Russians as the Yak-18 and under license by the Chinese as the Nanchang CJ-6, variations of this aircraft were the primary trainers for pilots of those countries during the late 1940s through the late 1960s, although a newer variant is still being produced today.

*Opposite:* The cowl flaps of this Yak can be clearly seen. The owner is Jack Wooten, one of many pilots who chose the Yak because of its hardy construction and cheap price for a warbird.

*Below:* This Nanchang, painted with a camouflage scheme, was shown by pilot Jason Griffin at the Wings of Freedom Airshow in Red Wing, Minnesota.

# Modern Times:
# The Airbirds Rule

# Modern Times:
# The Airbirds Rule

Although warbirds played critical roles after World War II in Korea and Vietnam, the period from 1947 until the collapse of the Soviet Union in 1991 found an emphasis on developing aircraft that could deliver nuclear weapons anywhere in the world. This period saw the development of Consolidated's ten-engine (six piston, four jet) B-36 Peacemaker, the B-52 Stratofortress, and the Boeing B-47, the first U.S. strategic bomber.

But many similar aircraft were killed on the drawing board by both the United States and the Soviet Union after the introduction of surface-to-air missiles—better known as SAMs. Even one of the most famous U.S. spy planes, the U-2, which could fly at heights of eighty thousand feet, was supposedly shot down by a Soviet SAM in 1961, although the circumstances surrounding that event remain a mystery even today.

As missile defense systems continued to advance after 1970, aircraft designers began to put more and more emphasis on maneuverability and sudden acceleration rather than pure speed. The star of this class was clearly the Lockheed Martin F-16, which first hit the skies in 1977 and has yet to ever be shot down!

To better protect their warbirds from SAMs, the United States also began to work on a program that was initially considered impossible—to build fighters and bombers that could go undetected on enemy radar. But by the early 1980s, the United States introduced the first stealth fighter, the Lockheed F-117, and the first stealth bomber, the Northrup B-2.

It was the F-117 stealth fighter that launched the American-led Operation Desert Storm in 1991. The war to free Kuwait from an invasion by neighboring Iraq was the first war in which warbirds clearly ruled the day. No one disputed that this war was truly won through the air. Other aircraft heroes during Desert Storm included F-15 Eagles, F-14 Tomcats, F-16 Falcons, F-18 Hornets, and

B-52 bombers. The war was over in less than a week!

After the terrorist attack on America on September 11, 2001, the United States responded with an invasion of Afghanistan to eliminate the terrorists, their training camps, and the Taliban regime that was harboring them. Whereas only 10 percent of the bombs employed just ten years earlier in the first Persian Gulf War were guided, 50 percent of the barrage unleashed by American aircraft in Afghanistan were guided weapons. This allowed the United States to significantly reduce civilian casualties. Unmanned aerial vehicles (UAVs) also played their first important wartime role here by tracking the terrorists and orbiting above the battlefield. When the time was right, these drones called in the big boys—the B-52s.

The Predator drones also provided a valuable role in the Iraq War of 2003 by providing real-time images of Iraqi troop movements. The Iraqi antiaircraft weapons could not reach the B-52s or target the Stealth B-2s or F-117s. U.S. air superiority in Iraq was so enormous that no Iraqi aircraft even took to the air!

Critical to so many U.S. missions since World War II has been the supercarriers. The star of today's supercarrier fleet is the USS *Nimitz*, named after Chester Nimitz, commander of the U.S. Pacific Fleet in World War II. Commissioned on May 3, 1975, this nuclear-powered giant has a crew of 3,200, a fleet of eighty-five planes, and a flight deck of 4.5 acres. From the mighty *Nimitz* featured in this spread, 6,500 missions commenced in support of Operation Iraqi Freedom.

As we look to the future of warbirds, it can almost be said that the sky is no longer the limit. Military space planes similar to the space shuttle are being designed for reconnaissance tasks and even attack missions. In the years to come, the warbirds, in whatever new forms they may take, will dominate any major military conflict.

Type: antitank and forward air
   control (FAC) aircraft
Maker: Fairchild
Country: USA
Powerplant: two 9,068-lb-
   thrust General Electric
   TF34-GE-100 turbofans
Max. Speed: 424 mph at
   sea level
Range: 550 mi
Service Ceiling: 34,695 ft
Max. Weight: 47,399 lbs
Armament: one General
   Electric GAU-8/A 30mm
   cannon plus up to
   16,000 lbs of weapons;
   FAC load consists of up to
   12 LAU-68 seven-tube
   rocket pods, two AIM-9
   Sidewinder air-to-air
   missiles, and electronic
   countermeasures
   (ECM) pod
Wingspan: 57 ft 6 in
Length: 53 ft 4 in
Height: 14 ft 8 in
Crew: 1

*Above:* The awesome firepower of the A-10 Thunderbolt starts with this 30mm seven-barreled Gatling-type cannon. This is the aircraft's main weapon against tanks. The cannon is so powerful that it can only be fired in short bursts, because it slows the aircraft down with its recoil!

*Below:* The Thunderbolt was named after another powerhouse, the World War II P-47 Thunderbolt. The modern Thunderbolt is often referred to as the A-10 Warthog because of its ungainly appearance. What started out its career as a tank buster has become an excellent Forward Air Control (FAC) airplane.

*Opposite:* Highly maneuverable, it can recover from a strafing run and be back on the attack quickly to support ground troops. Two planes can provide almost continuous coverage of the battlefield.

*Left:* The Harrier can fly at a stunning 662 miles per hour and then slow down until it is actually flying backward. It can also take off and land in a backyard with its revolutionary rotating jet ports.

*Opposite:* Two Harriers flying over the Miramar Airshow display a silhouette of the array of weapons available to the Harrier pilot. Those include Sidewinder missiles that make the Harrier formidable in a dogfight.

Type: attack
Maker: McDonnell Douglas
Country: USA
Powerplant: one 23,820-lb-
   thrust Rolls-Royce
   F402-RR-408 turbofan
Max. Speed: 662 mph
Range: 684 mi
Service Ceiling: 50,000 ft
Max. Weight: 31,000 lbs
Armament: one 25mm GAU-
   12/A Equalizer five-barrel
   cannon with 300 rounds;
   two AIM-9 Sidewinder
   missiles; provision for up
   to 13,228 lbs of bombs,
   rockets, or missiles
Wingspan: 30 ft 4 in
Length: 46 ft 4 in
Height: 11 ft 8 in
Crew: 1

*Below:* A modern-day version of the British Jump Jet, the amazing Harrier II is the U.S. Marine Corps' favorite aircraft for protecting ground troops.

Type: outsize cargo transport
Maker: Lockheed
Country: USA
Powerplant: four 43,000-lb-
 thrust General Electric
 TF39 turbofans
Max. Speed: 518 mph
Range: 6,320 mi
Service Ceiling: 30,300 ft
Max. Weight: 840,000 lbs
Armament: none
Wingspan: 222 ft 8 in
Length: 247 ft 10 in
Height: 63 ft 2 in
Crew: 7

*Above:* To say the Galaxy was as big as a house would not do it justice: this plane is as big as an apartment building. To operate a fully loaded Galaxy is like lifting nine fully grown humpback whales into the air and flying them at five hundred miles an hour from Los Angeles to London.

*Left:* The C-5 can open from both ends to load tanks and helicopters, and it can carry more than three hundred tons! It can deploy 360 fully equipped paratroops.

*Opposite:* You need to go up two flights of stairs to get to the cockpit of the plane. Even though the plane is huge, it's not that hard to fly. There are now even bigger Russian Antonov transports, but for twenty years the C-5 was the biggest plane in the world.

*Following pages:* The C-5 has twenty-eight wheels to support its massive weight, and landing gear that can "kneel" to accommodate the height of a truck bed for easy loading.

# C-130 HERCULES

Type: medium-range short
    takeoff and landing
    (STOL) transport
Maker: Lockheed
Country: USA
Powerplant: four 4,500-hp
    Allison T56-A-15
    turboprops
Max. Speed: 383 mph
Range: 2,350 mi
Service Ceiling: 28,000 ft
Max. Weight: 155,600 lbs
Armament: none
Wingspan: 132 ft 7 in
Length: 97 ft 9 in
Height: 34 ft 3 in
Crew: 3 to 5

*Above:* The Hercules has proven over the past fifty years to be a reliable performer and is now used by more than fifty air forces around the world. There are many variations of the plane and it has been used as everything from gunship to flying hospital.

*Left:* The pilots, navigator, and crew chief have a spacious cockpit to work in with more than three hundred lights, dials, switches, levers, and controls to monitor.

*Opposite:* The Hercules can carry more than nineteen tons of cargo and is capable of short takeoffs and landings. C-130s are deployed all over the United States but the best way to see one in action is to attend one of the free airshows put on by the U.S. military.

SEE INSIDE OF NOSE WHEEL WELL
FOR CONNECTION OF HINGED RADOME

Type: troop-carrying
    military helicopter
Maker: Boeing-Vertol
Country: USA
Powerplant: two 1,870-hp
    General Electric T58-GE-16
    turboshaft engines
Max. Speed: 159 mph
Range: 618 mi
Service Ceiling: 16,990 ft
Max. Weight: 24,300 lbs
Armament: none
Rotor Diameter: 50 ft
Length: 84 ft 4in
Height: 16 ft 8 in
Crew: 4

*Above:* The Sea Knight requires two pilots and can ferry up to twenty-five troops into battle.

*Opposite:* Windows below the pilots allow them to position the aircraft into precise placement. The Sea Knight is also used for search-and-rescue operations and snatching troops off to safety from the battlefield.

*Below:* As seen here in a demonstration of MAGTF (Marine Air-Ground Task Force), soldiers deploy out of the helicopters to secure the runway during the Miramar Airshow.

Type: fighter/attack
Maker: Lockheed
Country: USA
Powerplant: two General
    Electric F404
    nonafterburning engines
Max. Speed: 684 mph
    (estimated)
Range: Unlimited with
    air refueling
Service Ceiling: unknown
Max. Weight: 52,500 lbs
Armament: variety of bombs
    and missiles internally
    depending on the mission
Wingspan: 43 ft 4 in
Length: 65 ft 11 in
Height: 12 ft 5 in
Crew: 1

*Above:* "They never knew what hit them" applies very well to the Nighthawk. Known as the "Stealth Fighter," the F-117 is the world's first operational aircraft designed to work with low-observable stealth technology.

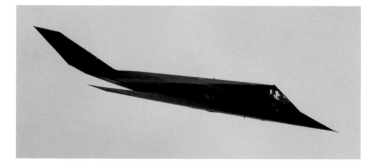

*Above:* The Nighthawk's unique butterfly tailplanes act as both elevators and rudders. The tail was designed to provide the least amount of radar reflections and to hide the engine exhaust from view.

*Opposite:* Seen here at the Miramar, California, Marine Corps Air Station during the Miramar Airshow, the Nighthawks make their home at Holloman Air Force Base in New Mexico. Your best chance of seeing one in person is at a major military airshow.

*Left:* Personnel of the Black Knight Squadron run a systems check on the landing gear of a Hornet. The squadron is preparing to be deployed overseas. When that happens, everybody goes—pilots, power line crews, repair specialists—an entire crew travels to wherever the planes go, whether it is on land or aboard a carrier.

Type: carrier-based naval
    strike fighter
Maker: McDonnell Douglas
Country: USA
Powerplant: two 16,020-lb-
    thrust afterburning General
    Electric F404-GE-400
    turbofans
Max. Speed: 1,190 mph
    (Mach 1.8)
Combat radius: 659 mi
Service Ceiling: 50,000 ft
Max. Weight: 49,225 lbs
Armament: one Martin
    Marietta M61A1 20mm
    Vulcan cannon, two AIM-9L
    Sidewinder missiles,
    plus ordnance
Wingspan: 37 ft 6 in
Length: 56 ft
Height: 15 ft 3 in
Crew: 1

*Opposite:* The condensation of the air around this Hornet comes from a combination of pressure and temperature caused by the high speed of the aircraft passing through air with a suitable level of moisture. In other words, blast through the atmosphere with one of these babies and you are going to shake things up a bit.

*Left*: This Hornet comes with quite a sting: it can launch from a carrier, bomb a target, be a fighter escort, suppress enemy air defenses, do deep or close air support, and dogfight with the best enemy planes.

# INDEX